Memories of the Future

Memories of the Future

The Daybooks of Tina Modotti

Poems by Margaret Gibson

Louisiana State University Press
Baton Rouge and London
1986

Designer: Christopher Wilcox
Typeface: Times Roman
Typesetter: G & S Typesetters, Inc.
Printer: Thomson-Shore, Inc.
Binder: John Dekker and Sons, Inc.

LIBRARY OF CONGRESS CATALOGING-IN-PUBLICATION DATA

Gibson, Margaret.
  Memories of the future.

  1. Modotti, Tina, 1896–1942—Poetry.   2. Photography—
Poetry.   I. Title.
PR9199.3.G49M45   1986   811'.54   85-23668
ISBN 0-8071-1308-5
ISBN 0-8071-1309-3 (pbk.)

Publication of this book has been supported by a grant from the National Endowment
for the Arts in Washington, D.C., a federal agency.

Some of these poems have appeared in the following magazines, sometimes in slightly
different form: *Clockwatch Review*, *Crazy Horse*, *Embers*, *Graham House Review*,
Iowa Review, *Michigan Quarterly Review*, *Minnesota Review*, *New England Review/
Bread Loaf Quarterly*, and *Parnassus*.

Cover photograph of Tina Modotti by Edward Weston
© 1981 Arizona Board of Regents
Center for Creative Photography

The author is grateful to the heirs of Antonio Machado for permission to quote from
and translate his poetry.

This book is for Joshua and Megan

Contents

Preface and Acknowledgments   ix
Tina Modotti: A Chronology   xiii

Memories of the Future   1
Doctrines of Glass and Wood   3
The Kiss of Our Parents   6
Fire Doesn't Die   9
Doors, Opening as They Do . . .   12
Fast Light   15
Darkroom Nights   18
In the Market   20
Still Lives   22
Vocation   24
Soledad   26
Día de los Muertos   28
What Love Is   31
Outcast   32
Maria   34
Madrid   36
From a Single Center . . .   39
Retreat to the Future   42
Home   45

Notes to the Poems   47
Glossary   51

Preface and Acknowledgments

"That's the Italian actress Tina Modotti," said the instructor as an afterthought into the dark of the room. He was referring to an image projected on the screen in black and white from the silent film *Greed*— a young mother brooding by the bed of her sick child, an image for the impotence and frustration of poverty and wordless grief. That was in 1968. I would not recall the face or name of Tina Modotti for many years, not until I read the few pages about her in Pablo Neruda's *Memoirs* in 1980. She had been, he said, a photographer in Mexico in the 1920s, a companion to Edward Weston. Neruda had met her in Spain in the 1930s during the Civil War; as a member of the 5th Regiment and as a nurse, she had worked with devotion and conviction. She had, he said, thrown her camera into the river in Moscow, abandoning art for political work.

A dramatic gesture—perhaps a fictitious one. I was to learn that Tina Modotti's was a life that had survived years of rumor and myth, years when she was no more than a portfolio of misplaced negatives, a mess of letters in a file, an abandoned journal, a face or a name in daybooks or histories written by men who had known her or seen her. Some spoke of her work; most remembered her great beauty, her many lovers, the political notoriety. *The Daybooks of Edward Weston*, published in 1961, included entries with information about Modotti and some of the portraits of her that he had made.

Who was Tina Modotti? Mildred Constantine, who undertook her biography, and Vittorio Vidali, Comandante Carlos of the 5th Regiment and Tina's companion for many years until her death in 1942, have done much in their more recent books to sift fact from rumor and myth. And yet there remain questions. Vidali speaks of her mysterious silence.

When I was following the life of Tina Modotti and reading histories of Mexico and Spain, I was also working in New London, Connecticut, in the Puerto Rican community. My friends there were Puerto Rican, Mexican, Chilean. I was learning to speak Spanish and hearing about the history of current political struggles in Mexico, El Salvador, Nicaragua, Chile, and Puerto Rico from those who had lived there. In that community, it was not difficult to make connections between many of the political themes and issues of Modotti's day and our own. The tension I experienced between my work as a poet and my work in the tenants' union at a housing project I felt to be provocative and creative, and as my interest in Modotti and my feeling for this community fed each other I came to know that I would write about Tina Modotti, this woman who had learned to live single-mindedly, who through a series of dramatic historical and radical personal transformations had lived according to her vision and in accord with principles that put her on the side of the poor and the oppressed.

Her photographs take essentially ordinary objects or working-men and women as their focus—a field of corn, the rims of wine-glasses massed together, doorways, streets, markets, a young Mexican reading a newspaper, hands at rest on the handle of a shovel, hands washing clothes, telephone wires, workers carrying bananas or crossbeams, women with large gourds on their heads, puppets, Mexico's street children, a still life—stark, iconographic—of a hammer and sickle against a muted background. For years lost or neglected, Modotti's photographs can be seen now at the Museum of Modern Art in New York City, at the George Eastman House in Rochester, New York, at the Philadelphia Museum of Art, and at the Center for Creative Photography in Tucson. They are beginning to receive the attention they deserve and are being exhibited more widely. The photographs communicate a powerful dignity and simplicity and integrity—qualities intrinsic to Modotti herself.

History, when retold, is of course revised history; biography relies on intuition and imagination as well as on document and fact. *Memories of the Future* is neither biography nor history, though I have made use of both. *Memories of the Future*, as a book of poems, is a creative revision, an indirect translation of the life of Tina Modotti. The poems are drawn from daybooks I imagine Tina Modotti to have kept during the last year of her life in Mexico City. At times she did keep journals, and she once wrote a poem following the death of her first husband. And so I imagine her in 1941 writing prose entries in her journals in one of the small rooms on the fifth floor of Calle Dr. Balmis 137 or on the *azotea* of that house from which she could see the city sprawling out toward the horizon and the volcano Popocatépetl in the distance. Made more solitary by a serious heart condition that would claim her life early in 1942, she writes in the spirit of *querencia*, a gazing back through the distance toward home, toward various points of origin, when she had once again shaped a new life for herself or had it shaped in postrevolutionary Mexico, in the Soviet Union, and in the struggles of Spain in the 1930s. I have "taken" the poems from those imagined daybooks. I have included a Chronology and at the back of the book Notes with relevant information about her life and its historical context.

In July, 1981, I went to Mexico to visit some of the places Modotti had lived during the years 1923–1930 and 1937–1942. At Calle Dr. Balmis 137, I climbed the dark stairs to the rooftop apartment, catching my breath from the heat and the ascent. In Panteón Dolores, I found Modotti's grave. In the flat gravestone itself, on which is carved her face in profile and the opening lines of a poem by Neruda about her, there is a small well at the base for flowers. It was filled with rainwater. In that primitive vase, someone had recently placed a single blue flower, taken from a full bouquet I saw on a nearby grave. Someone who perhaps had known Tina Modotti or her work had been there and had borrowed the flower to pay homage. These poems are somewhat like the flower left on her stone that damp afternoon in July in Mexico City.

For their generous assistance in helping me to learn about Tina Modotti, I want to acknowledge Mildred Constantine and Vittorio Vidali, whose books are the principal biographical sources—respectively, *Tina Modotti: A Fragile Life* (1975, 1982) and *Retrato di Donna Tina Modotti* (1982). I am particularly grateful to Mildred Constantine for information and photographs from her files and for spending time answering questions so graciously. Vidali, now deceased, answered letters and sent me his book from Trieste at a time in his life when his health was failing. If I cannot thank him now directly, I would like to honor the memory of his vigorous life. I am also grateful to the following people for their comments on the poems, for their help in translating Italian or Spanish, or for their help with photographs, source materials, even cameras:

Joanne Barkan, James Coleman, Robert Colodny, Connie Cook, Marta Daniels, Donald Davidson, Yvonne Días, Lillian Morales Fletcher, Jon Friedman, Milagros Guzman, Joan Hall, Edwin Honig, Jacqueline Janes, Joseph Levy, David McKain, Hobart and Jean Mitchell, the Museum of Modern Art's Photography Staff, Kay Mussell, Linda Pastan, Stephanie Strickland, and Dabney Stuart. I wish to thank Yaddo Corporation for its hospitality in the summer of 1982. Mildred Constantine kindly provided a negative of Edward Weston's photograph of Tina Modotti which appears on the cover. I would like to thank Lisa Rosen for her fine work with that negative. A grant from the Roger F. Murray Teaching Foundation at Phillips Academy/Andover has made possible the use of the photograph, and for that grant I am deeply grateful.

Tina Modotti: A Chronology

August 16, 1896   Named Assunta Adelaide Luigia Modotti, Tina is born in Udine, the capital of Friuli, in Italy, to Giuseppe and Assunta Modotti. She is the second daughter in a large family, her father a carpenter.

1911   Giuseppe Modotti immigrates to San Francisco, California.

1913   Tina immigrates to San Francisco, joining her sister Mercedes and her father.

1917   She marries Roubaix de l'Abrie Richey, "Robo," a painter and a poet. With him she moves to Los Angeles, where she works in silent films.

1921   She begins a love affair with Edward Weston, a photographer.

1922   Robo dies of smallpox in Mexico City; a month later, Giuseppe Modotti dies.

July, 1923   She leaves for Mexico to live with Edward Weston. They settle outside Mexico City in Tacubaya, moving into the city soon after.

1923–1926   She learns the camera, exhibits photographs, travels with Weston to photograph primitive and religious artifacts for Anita Brenner's book *Idols Behind Altars*. She joins a revolutionary union formed by Diego Rivera and David Alfaro Siqueiros, El Sindicato de Técnicos, Pintores, y Escultores (the Syndicate of Technical Workers, Painters, and Sculptors).

1926   When Weston returns to California, she remains in Mexico, making her living as a photographer.

1927   She joins the Communist party of Mexico and demonstrates against the executions of Sacco and Vanzetti.

1928   She becomes the companion of Julio Antonio Mella, a law student exiled from Cuba, then under the dictatorship of Gerardo Machado. She joins Hands Off Nicaragua, an anti-imperalist group.

January 10, 1929   She is at Mella's side when he is shot to death on the street as they walk home together in the evening. Afterwards, she participates in the protests and demonstrations directed against the murder, enduring the subsequent publicity and scandal that accompanied the attempted political cover-up. The assassins were hired by Gerardo Machado in Cuba.

1929   In Mexico City she exhibits her photographs, which are described by Siqueiros as works of faultless artistic and political consciousness.

1930   Falsely accused of an assassination attempt against the Mexican president, she is exiled from Mexico. Denied entry into the United States by Ambassador Dwight Morrow unless she give up her political views and unable to enter Italy safely because of the fascist dictatorship there, she sails on a Dutch ship to Europe.

1930–1936   She lives briefly in Germany, studies and works in Moscow and in Paris for International Red Aid, a branch of the Communist International which aided the families of imprisoned Communists. She becomes the companion of Vittorio Vidali, a professional revolutionary and a friend since 1927 in Mexico.

1936–1939   She joins the 5th Regiment in Spain, one of the International Brigades fighting in defense of the Second Republic after the Insurrection led by Franco and the Generals. She works as a nurse in Madrid's Workers Hospital and on various fronts throughout the Spanish Civil War.

1939–1942   She lives in Mexico City at Calle Dr. Balmis 137 with Vittorio Vidali (Comandante Carlos of the 5th Regiment) and works in the Antifascist League of Giuseppe Garibaldi. She returns to work briefly with the camera. The political climate in Mexico mirrored the struggles worldwide, a ferment of profascist and antifascist groups seeking power.

January 5, 1942   She dies of a heart attack alone in a taxi cab as she returns home from dinner with friends, and she is buried a few days afterwards in Panteón Dolores. Lurid speculations about her death were published in the newspapers, although these were shortly silenced by a poem published by Pablo Neruda, then ambassador to Mexico from Chile, who had known Tina in Spain.

Memories of the Future

Memories of the Future

1 January 1941

I've heard it said we choose our own deaths.
In all the chaff that fills us, the clean seed glows
and will explode at the right time.

That seems a pretty thought to put beside a corpse,
rude comfort—a hot water breakfast
for a hungry child. There are men who live
wistfully dead, wanderers who walk the streets
gently beneath a smothering blue. They put on
their clothes in the morning, remove them at night,
put them on in the morning. . . . For them
to choose to die is a birth.
                                        I know a different dead—
those the fascists shot in the working-class streets.
Drenched in oil to kill the smell, they were left
on display. Women swollen with child were forced
to drink petrol, men to dig their own graves.
Their wives had to watch, wearing signs:
I married a Bolshevik. Did these die at the right time?
And the wounded, slowly those with no breath
left to come gasping in bubbles of blood—these, too?

If we choose our own deaths, we choose all of it—
the kiss of our parents, our bodies, doctrines,
dark rooms. All of it our will. As an immigrant
I saw the coastal horizon move towards me, a clear
green line. I signed my name there—yes,
I said. I will be . . . and I chose it. Then moment
by moment I remembered and forgot as the future
moved towards me, through me, past—dimly, then
more dimly remembered. We choose our end.

But when we get there, do we know it?

I wanted a life plainly used, transparent. The ones
close to me, could they not see? Seeing,

1

could they not know more than I could in words
express? Silence is nearest to trust.
Now since the war in Spain—

                        bad dreams.

A man in a black shirt extends his hand, in his palm
a tear so hard no hammer can smash it, no sickle
slice through. Alarmed by darkness, heartworn
I tell each face that invades my sleep—

Join love and power, then you can never be hurt.

Once I thought—
into the poverty of darkness the moon casts her lot,
radical, beautiful. Our lives can be.

Doctrines of Glass and Wood

5 January 1941

In my memory, light shifts distances about,
faces wash in a shimmer of light that's not sun.
In one of these memories
                                    the wind furrows deep
sea channels out to the open sea. Papa's there,
the ridges of Friuli and Caldori north in the distance.
We turn past Venice, past a cemetery wall, towards
islands, villages, boats bobbing like bits of *cristallo*
on a sea glass backed by silver. Above Murano
smoke from the glass factories hangs low.

I recall
faces in an orange light of furnaces,
clay pots like beehives, a water trough, and balls
of fire rolled, pressed, cajoled and tricked into fine
docility by enormous men. Fire doesn't die—
it is the glare of strong hearts. But it can be thinned.
I watched Benvenuto—my uncle a hero—take a gather
of glass from the molten pot and blow, and in three blows
a red pear grew on imprisoned air. It was a dancer
stretched, an orchard of myriad things, all possible—
then rolled on a marver, thrust on a block and blown
deep red into a mold, and clamped there. It set
a moment only, and when the mold was opened, there—

a globe . . .

taken by tongs to the lehr for its slow journey through
that tunnel, annealing with time, a tiny world
deceptively cool, taught seemliness, given limits,
made single—an individual thing, and real—
or so it seemed. But Benvenuto mocked the mold.

"The glass was on fire," he said. "But it wasn't free."

3

Intended for the tables of the rich, the glass might be set
like a helmet of breath over orchids and pearls.
It might glitter at the Savoy, a hotel in London
flooded once so the guests might eat as if in Venice,
floating in imported gondolas while jeweled black men,
like sconces, held fire up on thin glass candlesticks.

Benvenuto told me this—he was a set of lungs,
a set of muscle. No more? Perhaps, he spat,
an alchemist on wage.

What did I then know of anger? I was six. I saw
glassblowers shape with their breath glowing forms,
each shimmering sphere like a life. Into the light
by their stems I wanted to hold them, glass
after glass blown for milk or wine or the hours—
a cluster of roses, transparent in the light.

Of me alone, Papa asked—
Who are you? What have you done? What more
can you give? For whom are you poor enough?—
until the questions had dignity, and my life,
which was to answer in work, had a chance
at dignity, might build something new.
He was a carpenter, these questions
his plumb line and rule.

As a child, I was his partner. I cleaned his tools,
I walked with him to work, to look for work.
In the midday trattorias he hummed violin, I danced
on the bare wood table, a tiny child buoyant in
smoke and sunlight, in the smell of sweat and basil
and bread sure of the sane, undemanding love
I sensed there, a strength basic as polenta,
natural as rain.

                              In him I saw the power
to build—in brick and stone and wood. I learned
to wonder how a man could do good work, the work
required by others, and feel betrayed. He was hurt
by work, and by the lack of work. Who respected him?
We never framed that question.

In wine and May Day parades, in the theater of the streets
I saw him briefly heal. He joined love and power.
And whether he whistled Puccini or turned Hegel
on his head and tweaked his toes, he had a value,
and he knew it.

But in his face the fractures deepened,
and the craze lines of blind self-sacrifice beneath his eyes
spread in a silent heat. His eyes were haunted.
They watched me—watching as the years took
my body into new geographies, as the years stretched us
farther apart, a slow journey. He followed a desperate
migration, west, to a new world I could barely imagine,
shimmering—warm with work and yellow sunlight.

The Kiss of Our Parents

9 February 1941

Class makes us spectators
of each other—also sex. But how could I know
I'd find my beauty in his face as his hands
uncovered me, his hands hungry for the touch
of family—two years homesick in San Francisco,
please, he said that first morning, the dust
of the train still on me, the smell of ocean and salt
still in my blood, the future still field after field
after field's stretching the eye over a leap of continent
to find Papa, waiting—then he sat on the edge
of my bed, his hands uncovered me. In the silence
his face spoke, saying *please*. I turned to the wall,
felt for a moment his breath on my neck.
Then my sister came running in.

In the silk factory I worked—the stuff
that makes a good kimono sweep across skin like oiled
light on water, making a girl's breasts swell
in the secret curve of new cocoon cloth—the raw silk
reeled to skein, woven to warp and woof, boiled
milk white and weighted with mineral salts—
that was beauty to me.
                              It swelled my fingers red,
I itched. Whole days went milky. I boiled off
the sericin, melting from threads the cocoon glues,
freeing the silk of dreams. And I drifted,
drifted back to Mamma's voice—*Piensa de otros*,
think of others, she said. Words I heard in Italian,
the room dark as the cave of a child's empty belly.
Piensa de otros, as the next shift of children
climbed up the one bed, and the others moved
to sleep on the floor, making the fact of others
light that dark universe, our room. When there was
food, our first delight was to see it, in Mamma's
basket purple eggplants, perfectly formed string beans.

6

Italy's songbirds we memorized—first stroke
the feathers, smooth the colors, learn their silk
while the water for plucking them boiled.

Join love and power? I worked two years in silk
to help bring Mamma and our family home.
I joined Papa in the theater of our district's café
lights. I lived in the mirror of his face,
thinking, reflection is a woman's place.
I gave back his need to know he'd made
something beautiful—he wasn't a guildsman
of old Venice, honored for the objects he'd made—
a vase, a bridge, a lion on the lintel of a door.
He couldn't walk to the city's center and touch
softly the bronzes or the bells he'd cast.
So he touched, or wanted to, me—and felt
the accidents of class and work and loss
of homeland lighten.

But what was I?

And in that mood of innocent betrayal, I married
Robo, an artist, gentle as a velvet coat.

In Hollywood, in the city of angels, Los Angeles,
at sunrise each morning I invented my face
for the Studio. I was their rose, an Italian dusk—
a free woman in the pure arc of downfall.
The director ran his finger along the silk
of my collarbone, he moved his lips without sound.
Wanting to please became an art. In Studio
portraits, I was a curve of breast, a head
tilted up, sleek skin and silk, an accolade of gauze.
The camera was my exacting lover, I the fate
of beauty in the world—two bit parts.

A dancing girl whose head was a sultan's footstool,
a mother too poor to buy food for the child
feverish on the cot beside her—thus,
in Stroheim's *Greed*, I stared off into nowhere,
beautiful, my hair slightly mussed.

Fire Doesn't Die

7 March 1941

Yesterday I was drawn
by this season's first light rain to a café
on the plaza. *Salud*, said a stranger, pausing by my table.
He sold me a rose and a small round of bread. I smelled
the rose, I ordered wine—a glass for myself and a glass,
as is custom, for the unknown guest who might,
out of the hubbub of guitars and parrots, come sit with me
and be still.
          And then I saw, firm as memory,
a fine mirage. Robo *presente*! He was squinting, confused
by the uproar of Fords and crowds, *presente*,
stern and vague, with his usual book, the one with blank
pages, in hand. Almost I said, sit down. We'll take
wine together. We'll drink as before.

But he would not sit,
and I grew cold remembering the formal portrait
Weston made of him—a stance theatrical, hands
elegant, half Robo's face in shade. He'd cracked a door
so that he stood composed in a triangle of light,
a telling slant of light on the floor. The portrait
Robo held out for me to see shook in his hand.
He placed it quiet on the table, tracing over and over
that triangle of light with his thumb. "The two of you
are lovers," he whispered. "There's confession in the light."
A little sad, he smiled. "Look here." And it was true.

He turned even more to his paints and easel,
to mantras and blank pages in so blue a light
I couldn't follow. He wanted private horizons—
"Facts are not always beautiful," he wrote.
He wanted a world of rare delights in which beggars
gave their crusts to bright birds. By nature,
he couldn't possess. I was his glass of red wine,
sipped gently and gently set down. I was the rose

on his coat, admired. Worthy, but without
knowing why.

I wanted to be more visible—to see, to contemplate . . .
but I also wanted lilac wet with morning drawn
round and round my taut nipples. I wanted
the mystery women make with their bodies,
blood and milk. I thought I wanted freedom—
but I wanted to be used.

Primavera in Friuli, I was the last to notice
first green, blind until all the grazing field
swept tidal, sea-fire green, though the shoots
one by one had been there, gathering force
since solstice. Just so, until the afternoon,
alone with him, when Edward spilled saki
on my upturned hand, and took my palm—
bending close as if to read what that shudder
in my life-line said, and put his mouth there
instead (a pool of rice wine warm as semen,
clear as a lens) and drank, and my hand fired
like a cup in a kiln,
                    not until then
had I noticed how our casual glances one by one
had gathered to such a steady gaze that California's
hills and fields outside swept to full kindle of vine,
the sun a green blaze.
                  Robo was asleep
when I came home. No eyes to look into. Papa
felt near, just a notion of him there as I walked
about in the room, touched the pears in a bowl,
the shadows in the chest of paints. I lit a candle
in a dish. I stared as flame split the dark,
split it sheer. A chasm opened,
and I stretched my hands to its light—in part
to warm them, in part to block the heat—

then raised hands and arms up over my head
in the spire divers make as they arch . . .
before the plunge,
                    a moment's hesitation,
balanced on the edge of a depth so pure I seemed
to choose, without sounding it, free fall into fire—
swept by fire.

Doors, Opening as They Do . . .

27 March 1941

"I think I ought to begin to do some work, now
I'm beginning to see. . . ." Robo left these words
on the kitchen table, Rilke's words copied in black
and gold script—an apricot, unripe, set on the page
as a weight. Join me when you are ready,
the apricot meant. Elegant words: "One ought to wait
and gather sense and sweetness a whole life long,
a long life if possible." If possible. I began to see
a pampered man, that Rilke, a silk smoking jacket,
a mauve cravat, a table of mahogany mirror
in which reflect many cities, men and things,
a surge of wings, and a heart's blue iris, the petals
unwinding in slow pirouettes. Beyond his window
laborers like Papa sweat, while on the other side
of many white rooms a woman has her life
invented for her—white, white.

"One must have memories, many nights of love . . ."
and childbed and deathbed, windows never shut
against wind, a long spool of road to unwind through
bright hills, the sea in storm, monumental skies
and stars—in short, one must live.

A week in Mexico, Robo wrote how doorways,
opening as they do from the public street
into gardens of green willow and wine bougainvillea,
charmed him—such intimate exposures that he wished
for a door in his chest—he'd let a lover in
past the veil of fruit trees to watch three gulls
carouse at the lip of a well, and that well a deep
door down to the sea. A man could drift,
casual petal down that well, and float for centuries,
the centuries could float in glass-bottomed boats,
we two alone with them reviewing undersea roses
and the arbors of bone and the light that rises

12

from such bones. That same light shimmered
from the page as I read. I called it his despair.

Then he died. He didn't have dark theories
or see cities collapse into fields, and the fields
smear with rumor. Younger than I he remains,
leaving for me only a moment on the train
when a telegram was put in my hand—I was going
to him. He'd died, it said, alone, the final words
on his tongue blurred in the heat, a page torn
from his journal tight in his hand. So they said—
I never saw, except in dreams, that door swing
open on its hinges to the empty chair by the empty bed,
the plants in their clay pots unwatered. Mexico's
campesino sun, the long river of martyr's blood
that warms beneath the fields, gold birds
that oversee the *maíz*—these were not for him.
His sun was a dove of the silver mist,
a seamless, perfect shell, pale blue—
his hand a cold nest.

Once there in Mexico,
in the young afternoon only hours past his burial,
I stood on the street at a doorway, looking in.
I let doorjamb, threshold, and lintel frame
a woman on her knees patting tortillas.
Like butterflies her hands moved soft, her courtyard
savory with earth and lime, soaked *maíz* and woodfire.
Between one *maguey* and a loop-eared cactus
chickens scratched. Her man stacked *ollas*
for the market. It was all there:
one moment shining, impersonal.
I wanted to hold each detail. I wanted time
to stand still. I wanted soul to be sun
as only the sun can be, warm in the murmur

of doves, fresh in the folds of a just washed, pale
yellow coverlet. The moment passed.
She stirred a pot of beans, he finished work
and sank into siesta against the wall, his serape
wrapped about him like a wave from the sea.

That moment I was apprenticed, I was changed.
I went home to learn the camera, back to Weston,
changed. I would bring him to Mexico. Meanwhile
on the train, I slept in a homely smell of milk, warm
tortillas in the basket at my feet, across from me
a *campesina*, her bundle of child slung tight in her shawl.
Out the window,
                    tierra caliente: hot land, blue hills,
sun like a giant *comal*—and in my dreams a woman
held a ball of fire in her hands without pain or harm,
bending over a vast bowl as she shaped the fire,
squeezing, as if she were washing a towel or
kneading dough on a heated stone, Indian-style.
Though her eyes were blank and blind,

she showed me the work I'd chosen.

Fast Light

5 May 1941

Last night
on the *azotea* I watched the west of the city
flash and burn its fiesta—cannonades,
mescalito songs, great wheels of light
that dye the midnight orange and rose. Madrid,
I thought—Madrid! the street in flames, days
and nights on my feet, in the hospital stumbling
about the kitchen and the halls stripping sheets
and the dead—anything not to sleep,
anything not to dream.

I remembered Edward. In last night's splendor
he'd have seen only a rain of stars—
and they were there. In Mexico, as anywhere,
the dream has mists of gold to envelop you,
and you go in gold, arms outstretched,
to feel your way through pyramids of onion,
chiles, papayas, *aguacates*, white walls
of calla. For you think the tree of life
has tumbled from its distant constellation
down in a tropical rain—more fire
than rain—masking hills with green and lupine,
filling lakes with hyacinths, clouds
with lilies. In this ecstasy you see
mere silhouettes for the men and women
who daily go in grief to the vendors of small
white coffins in a heap. Or you see that wood
and call it the natural pruning of a primitive life.
In Mexico, the rain of stars can be
the sting of sweet evasion in the soul.

With Edward,
                it was fast light, sudden twilight,
darkroom nights. Between living and dreaming
he loved a whitewashed solitude
to which I'd run barefoot in the rain,

my kimono open. The room would fill—a cot,
an old wool flowered cloth, blue jar, fine light.
In the slow, slow thrum of our bodies we'd come,
whispering, "I'm not moving, not moving."

I'd wash prints at noon, and sense . . .
something amiss. A beggar's gaunt face,
that could bring the mood, or the cluster of
roses I'd arranged, four buds unfolding in stillness,
clitoral—the body's female clock.
Such riches, poverties—either one
might thin in the chemical wash of the tray,
so much less than I'd meant. Then I'd quit,
I'd help cook, I'd lie in the sun, sealed off,
a stone. *Estoy un poco triste hoy*—I'm sad,
I'd say, and walk the *avenida* with my Graflex,
drawn to doorways, arches, stairs. Where
did they go? inside, through, down.
We are born in shadow, we live in a mist—
but I couldn't break through.

Afternoons in a glare of light impersonal as history,
I walked. I watched whole lives disappear.
Men and women of the barrio, they'd turn a corner,
miss a stair, enter silently a warp of air.
They weren't missed. So many of us have done it—
stepped over the drunk in the street,
turned away from the beggar on whose sordid red
stump a splurge of flies swirls like a dance of filings
drawn to a magnet. Such men have no future—
simply, they don't exist. *Whose world is this,*
I said—*Or mine or theirs, or is it none?*

And where did I live? In Edward's room?
in the street? In my own room I noticed
first, in dreams, random images—

in a yellow light I'd never seen I saw
a crowd of corn, notched bamboo, a mass of
sombreros for sale. Above a clot of huts on a hill
clouds lifted, weights that might fall
on a world too still to have people in it yet.
There was a contour to the silence. I knew
the streets would fill. I'd see their faces.
In the center of this pueblo there was a public
well, a rope to sink down it, a clay shard
near for drinking. The town might change—
should change; would.

I waited for the streets to fill.
But there were only a few baskets, red chiles,
reeds—no hand to weave them round.
In a window wind rasped the dried roots
strung there. Sometimes I heard numbers tallied,
like the names of the dead after battle.

Awake, I watched the sunlight. Slowly I began
to fill it. I photographed the corn in a field,
bamboo—each crowd of it weighty, real.
Each had a bruise of shadow, each was a refuge,
quiet.
        What I felt . . . I couldn't say it—

Why am I in such despair?

Darkroom Nights

7 May 1941

One night in Amecameca's Hotel Sacro Monte
I lay awake—the bed hard, the pillows white
with the geranium and stock we put there.
Mountains cold, moon aloof—Edward
shivered as he slept. I couldn't close my eyes.
I watched a chair cast ribs of shadow on the wall.
How well they kept their secrets, I thought—
the things of the world mute, patient.

The bed was a lumpy altar—
I had been worshiped there, lifted out
of myself, by the ecstasy of my specific female
flesh made goddess of the flowers, flush and open.
I was able to stop time, back to the first time
we'd touched—let it be always the first time,
Edward said. Sex is magical thinking—
water burns, flowers dawn in the stones.
The first time, in Glendale, he'd looked at me
first through the camera: an hour's delay,
glance as touch, and finally, finally touch—
a slippery transit, beyond all limits.

Was it magic, or skill, when he took me
naked on the *azotea*? in the sun shooting finished
photographs—decisive, my body a figure
of Aztec craft, every curve and cut made
with love and power joined in sure design.
I had a dignity delicate and fit.
Yet I'd dread it when he'd say,

                Come, Zinnia—
I'll shoot heads of you today.

Those days I lived as a man—that is,
wore jeans, smoked a pipe, refused to make
vows to my lovers. I was a willful solitude.
A doctor had said, You will never have children.

I could make no appeal—the doors in my cells
slammed shut. My body sealed, a tomb. I appeared
to be, and was not, a woman.
                                        I lived in the darkroom
of my body, mute of all light. My body had
betrayed me—or had it freed me?
I wondered, do we ever invent our lives? We yield,
or we rebel. When are we our own?

That night I waited for the moon to sink to dawn,
a glimmer of the irreconcilable just beginning
in the backlighting of my brain.

In the morning we climbed the volcanos. Below
stretched a mesa of level green and blankets of water
where hyacinths floated, above them clouds
of infinite muscle. I saw everything to scale—
how small we are. My questions hushed.
What I thought I was, I wasn't. What I thought
I knew, I didn't. What I wished to do,
I couldn't. I was single, a moment
alive in skin and bones,
simple seeing.

In the Market

1 July 1941

Mine must be still a decadent spirit.
Today on the street I ate a sugared coffin's
sugared child, and in one swallow Guanajuato's ground,
like a gunshot, opened. I was back in the *Panteón*
I'd toured with Edward, back with the dead.

I can't think what made us go.
With the taste of coffee still in our mouths,
we'd made love. With the straw pattern of the *petate*
imprinted on our skin, we'd washed in the sun.
Down the steps to the fusty vault, I felt his semen
leave me, wet on my thigh. Why would we have wanted
to see bones? That is, I'd expected bones,
not bodies warped in tight skins, in brown
naked hides. Not the scythe of grins, all flesh
made rind. And not the pod of a fetus with its empty
suck at a leathery breast. Edward said—
the ultimate still life, a monumental theme.
But I heard the baby smack its lips, and I fled.

I found myself in the market, touching onions one
by one. I traced silhouettes of shoots and calla stalks
on air, watched one bud split its caul and the white
spathe open. Cold, I let street life slip over me.
I searched each face, in each heard a dry, deathly
smack of the tongue. But I realized for the first time
power—the power to see a world buried in daylight.
I was a lens—and I saw.
                    There rose up for me
that day in Guanajuato's streets the dead and the living—
they breathed through my breath, they rinsed through
my pores their blind needs. They were hands
scrubbing clothes, they gripped shovels
and newspapers, lifted cones of bananas, carried
crossbeams on their backs. They went down in the mine

to a source like their mother—they danced in the dust's
brief abundance. Together they endured.

In the street a man shouted a drunken *vacilada*,
hermetic pain pulled inside out, mystical
and snickering like a mescal worm, laughter
that stabbed at the light. *Los muertos mueran,*
y las sombras pasan—the dead die, shadows pass.
But the air they breathed, we breathe. Their faces
backlight our own, our lives spring up
from their dreams—light
in the work of these thick city streets.

In the center of town I saw
an old rusted pump the color of ocher,
color of bloodstone, ancient as the channel of the vulva,
menstrual color. Near it an old woman in a black
rebozo stacked tortillas on a cloth, a *brasero*'s
charcoals glowed, and the old Ford motor
used for grinding the pueblo's corn chugged along.
There was a smell of oil, smoking meat.
I remember the water's iron taste—I used
two hands to pump it. I drank from a gourd.

I thought of lilies—how they pull water clear through
their green channels. In them was presence,
an ease of future. As for me, watching dark water
splash in the dust, wiping my wet chin on my sleeve,
washing my hands in the earth-colored wet—
I'd have struggle, *la lucha*.

Still Lives

7 July 1941

When Edward was gone from Mexico a year,
he sent me a still life of a shell. Against pitch-black
background so thick nothing else existed, there spun
a single whorled shell, chambered, a fiddlehead
or embryo furled like a musical note flung into space
or a windwhirled moon cut open.
It was perfect and lone, mystical, formal.
I admired how it shocked: inhumanly, no
opportunity to revise or remake it—we couldn't opt
for that, the way sentimental people will fret
what is out of their hands, stolen, buried.
It simply presented itself, like the heads of those
who know how they should be seen, heroic.

But who would see it? In whose world did the shell
exist? The museum romantic's? the saint's?
the silk salon's? Behind this shell, blank as black
outer space, the background yawned. If there were
suffering, it had no weight. If compassion, no root.
The shell floated free, from hunger, dust, and grief
entirely distant. In the barrios it would be only
an amulet held to the ear of one who chose to be lost
in the dim narcotic whisper of a sea. In that
lagoon of reprieve,
                              an invisible hand,
imperial in its greed, sharper than hunger, thrives.
It swills oil and ore and blood. The fascist
descends from it, he swims in the life-line river
of that hand's mighty cash flow. This hand
hires the Moor, twirls swastikas, bruises
the breasts of black women. It files the gold beaks
of a murder of crows, unbuttons sweat glands,
pries toenails and testicles, sows fear in the land.
This hand sweeps armadas of bombs on the barrios,
rises up in their smoke to smack down flat

the children in the street. Its fingers are Armco,
Esso, and Krupp.
                    This hand a still life obscures,
blank backgrounds hide. Soft focus blurs it
in halos of charity, circles of confusion, mirage.
Oo's and Ah's of the rich—for the hand is a patron.
It buys up our shells, our wineglasses, roses,
all our heroic heads.

Papa knew this hand,
its power to pluck his roots, count his hairs, tweeze
his veins and pull them taut or slack as strings—
then leave him, a dangle in the silent air, ridiculous
small fellow, a *títere*. Of the hand that blots
into background our lives, of the art that culls out
in beautiful focus a shell—
                    how can a single
small voice demand, For whom are we poor enough?
How many must say it . . . how long?

To Edward what could I say? I sent him
a portrait of two callas, against stucco pale
as dawn. The long stalks, as if grown together at the base
or held by a common root, curved like the graceful
necks of swans, the throats and blades of the blossoms
each tipped away from the other, bent on different
sources of light, as if there could be two suns.
I thought they evoked our separateness. And yet
there in the funnel of space the two callas made
was the dim silhouette of a third, evolving in air,
blown towards bloom. Together they were this riddle:

> *Between living and dreaming*
> *there's a third thing.*
> *Guess it.*

Vocation

16 August 1941

Me considero una fotógrafa y nada más.

I consider myself a photographer, nothing more.
I said that in the years I lived alone.
The words gave me focus, purpose. I never believed
the words. Subject to the violence of *things*,
the bourgeois man makes claims—I am *this*, or *that*,
or *this*—and he lives in that cramped prison, alone.
I lived as one free—a photographer in the morning,
communist in the afternoon. Nights I kept to wash
prints, watch stars, smoke and read—a silent time
to count gifts, the best ones
                                        danger, disillusion, failure—
gifts that say what you are, how you must
continue.
                Today, my birthday,
an old friend brought back to me old negatives.
We held them to the light. A child at a brown breast,
the technical focus: nipple. Other children
hungry in the dust—born empty, moved through
empty rooms to empty dust, to live or silently
die there.

My friend said, these are the best of you, Tina—
as if they were not children, but old skins
shuffled from a former self, as if we see
only ourselves when we look
"out there."
                I felt an unexpected
hush hold house and street, city, mountain,
and distance still. In the old days at home
when the family gathered, at times in the clatter
of dishes and in the spiral of voices rising,
a similar hush intervened—mysterious, tense.
In such a silence Mamma and Papa joked,
listen: a child's conceived.

In the negatives I held, I saw children remain
rooted—but I am the child of departures,
always the immigrant. What next? the unexpected.
What more? the loss of wanting to be more.
What power? longing.

Who is content to be witness only? Sometimes my chest
burned, urgent. I'd think then of Mamma's patience
and carry it, rain in a bowl, to the darkroom
where I worked.
              In Tehuantepec
campesinas carry on their heads wide gourds
painted with flowers, broad as moons. They glow
and wither and give seed. Rain fills them up—
in drought women walk to the river, the sun
hanging gold in their ears. What they know

as they wash ash and dust from their bodies,
as they fill gourds, and lift, and bear them home—
their feet falling sure, on dirt roads
retracing the steps of their mothers—what these women
know, *that*
              I wanted. I wanted to walk to the river
in the company of women powerful by nature.
I wanted the burning well in my chest to flow,

and someone drink.

Soledad

9 September 1941

When the room echoes in the morning, and air is dust,
when troubles shadow the floor where sun once
struck the *petate*, that's the time
to enter the body and stand firm there.
And if you're a woman,
                if you know
the man always leaves, as he came, by surprise—
walk out of the city alone and study land.
On it lemon twilights flash, then a furze of wild flowers,
red. Caught on the eyelid of the pond one moment,
the moon winks and goes. Rain collects in the field,
it is mud, it is worked into rows and rows. A hand
places seed corn or slings the beans out into drills.
It is not male or female, the land—but a power
preoccupied, inventive, free.

I have been with many men. This has nothing
to do with weakness, or with desire. More
with a kind of force, sensed blind. Out of nowhere
a man with a burning mission flares—*here*,
now—and the moment takes me under,
ground opens to a core of fire. . . .
What the body knows, I remember.

Our first day together, Mella and I, we watched
a woman weave. She wore the loom, tied to her waist
at one end, the other secured to a tree in the *alameda*.
"I am trying to see what I sense inside," she said.
She watched her hands at work—her hands moved
fast and full. And yet her eyes knew void.
Negrita,
        she was dark.

We sat and watched her weave—her eyes were pitiless,
objective, fixed. I didn't use the Graflex—how could
I photograph that look? She was cold and raw,

yet could have melted the lens—*fuego*, fire
her focus.

By afternoon, white threads flashed through,
and when the light was lower, finished,
Mella bought it for me, a gift.

Yesterday I unwrapped it from newsprint, a simple
red *rebozo*, a color of earth good for corn, a solitude
of red that sweeps unbroken until near the fringe
at one end a white bird soars, one wing unfinished,
its feathers raveling into the tassels, and from there
into wind as it goes.

I put it on. I put it on and wept.

What is the power of a man and a woman? Without
opposites that tend towards each other,
there's no will to live, no need
to heal.
      The oppressors have us.

Día de los Muertos

1 November 1941

Today, shadows laugh at death's circling
and at sexual longing—all hunger.
How fat is the city?
                    Fat. It lolls at crowded tables,
wears gunpowder, facepowder. Men who should be
massing their power—dance, until fat shakes loose,
their bones unlock. They dance *vacilada* and laugh—
and death returns it.

Nothing is lost, years ago Mella said—
his head flung back, his blood in the street
like a dare. Nothing is lost, I believed that.
Though for days after, my image for life
was a woman drinking wine from a funnel,
her feet inevitably red with the spill.

Was nothing lost? Still Mella lay on the pavement,
the wind blew. No sirens, but the moon rolled down
the street in a state of shock, the moon tumbling through
all its phases, full to new, like a broken clock. I ran
from car to car, from house to house. Mella bled
in the street, a man strolled into the library to find a book,
a woman scolded invisible children. I screamed . . .
but how peacefully he bled! his blood
sinking and joining rivers underground, the rivers
that dye corn red and feed and feed the future.
Wine red, he flowed there. Nothing is lost,
he said.

At his funeral, I was the dark one—
negrita cambuja—the one near the white stacks
of roses. Armband white, heart white as splinters
of bone in his ashes, I stood in a negative world,
blacks/whites reversed. No safe light,
no darkroom for work out of public view.

The body that had filled me, his body,
now filled an urn. Some of the ash I'd scattered
on the street his blood had stained, the rest
would be sent back to Cuba when we could.
In Cuba, the tyrant Machado sucked sugared
drinks through the long hot *tiempo muerto*.
I suffered dead time, too: time after *zafra*
or harvest, when hands hang down and hunger
has emptied all promises. Students struck
sparks from the discontent. In Cuba they cut
cables of the Electric Bond and Share—
these spat in the streets like imperial snakes.
News of the murder thickened in the air,
a smoke of fire not ready yet to burn clean.
Hurts smoldered.

Just the day before, I'd photographed him.
I hadn't washed the blood from my skirt.
I hadn't let them tint his cheeks. I thought—
let them see what they've done. He was cold
to touch, yet the illusion of breath-fire lingered.
Upside down on ground glass, the image of my lover
breathed stubbornly; he slept as I'd seen him
mornings. I had to shoot frame after frame
to believe him dead, identical frames, no new
angles, no tricks. *Dead* means you can't revise.
Dead means fixed. *Dead* means the stern prison
of form, beyond any love which rebels against
blunder, obstacle, hunger—these powers,
these *compadres* of the poor.
                            Alive means water,
means assuming the shape of the glass water fills,
but first shape the glass with your own deep breath.
Alive means will. For this is political alchemy—
make water burn. Make water burn what binds us,

make water burn what binds us transparent as glass,
make water turn wine in the glass.
This is *síntesis*,
among the last words on the page Mella left
in his typewriter. I photographed the words
and the machine whose keys had transported them
from his brain to flammable paper. Blank paper,
I went to his funeral. Soon they would write on me,
words of hate. I wanted to dawn—*madrugar*—
to see swift just revenge form like sun on the blank
scroll of the sea, and the sea unroll all its power
on the kill. But I was alone. I had no power for that.
I waited. I could feel only the surge of my own quiet
will redoubled. They could not move me.
They did not.

When the press called me *puta*, conspirator, spy—
for the fascists!—when they broadcast nudes of me
and said things, when they flayed bare skin
with their questions or used me like vodka,
they wanted what men of that kind always want—
a mirror for their own fingers at their own
secret parts. And when they were silent,
their silences hissed: Don't you know what love is?
Why is your uterus empty?

Don't you know what love is?

What Love Is

2 November 1941

Most of us
can only say I caught a glimmer of it once,
a light mere words find hard to come by, a silence
whose value rises in degree like dawn through a still sea
or like the candle lit in the green street stones when it rains—
then stone is matter raised in power, more itself.

Out the window now the moon's a rim of a polished cup,
its *pulque* poured out. Like the moon, a fraction of myself,
once I turned and turned, alone in the room, alone
in the city, alone—until walls blurred, edges
blurred. I dilated and cleared, spun round in total
revolution,
                no one to tell
I was empty or full, there, not there. . . .

Then I knew how the mystic's rose is shattered, its center
everywhere, distributed like corn and beans and guns—
rosetas, by the handfuls given out.
                          Any way you turn
it's one vision. When *look* is the work you do,
love is there, beyond good and evil, beyond talk—
which does not cook the rice, grind corn, or clear land.
Unless you talk this way—
                  say what you really want.

When I say *life*, for instance, I mean what's possible.
When I say *soul*, I mean the material bead of rain that hangs
from the margins of a storm. I mean what gathers and fills
and depends on a cross-fire balance of winds.
                       When I say
love, I mean what we've had and had to lose to be what we are.
I mean what continues without us, and somehow,
because.

Outcast

17 November 1941

North Americans don't understand
austerity of soul. They call it sorrow—soft,
a female dignity. They don't know how strong
it is. Beneath my eyes these shadows are ashes
of a birth. Once I wept in the sun and Edward
shot that track of a tear down my cheek.
I said nothing. My work then was to weep,
all my power stored in the darkroom's mute
instinctive chrysalis. But from such protections
love is charged to free us.

Mella and I,
we loved the Revolution more than any person—
always we said that. It gave each person value.
I said this in public and became a public scandal.
Was I human? a woman? I was a loaded gun.
In a year I was accused of crimes, imprisoned,
exiled—all unjustly. What could I do? Like him
I wore a death mask, dignified, composed.
I fasted.
            Stripped down to the fate of the poor,
my room to a moon, reduced to bare words
that eclipsed ghosts and furniture, foodstuff,
clay bowls, books—I was I.
An ability to work. A sudden shift of focus
inward to the body's own cells, prison cells—
and they were all on strike against greed,
against lies.

Yet in the boat off the coast, just exiled,
headed who knows where, denied access to any
I loved, then—I faltered.
I wanted only to die. I hated the future.
Mella had died as he was, *what* he was—
even his enemies knew.

Me no one knew. All borders closed—
they were deadlines. There was only one
grim passport I wanted. But then . . .

Listen to me.
If I have to build a road in the sea to reach you I will.
What we can think can be.

The words were Mella's.
In the charged grainy light of the sea they came
before dawn—a rush in my head,
in my heart a loud hum of blood.
I had been peeling an orange, the peel letting down
in a spiral to my lap, the scent of peel oils
sprayed on my skin. Then the fruit felt hot,
from the core it glowed. I was suddenly
empty, tense as a wireless before a message comes.
His words came then, as fast as I could hear.

I felt a new journey begin—why? to what end?
Unknown.
          But I'd agreed. I had a passport
stamped on the lines of transition in my palm.
I had a passport east, to the unknown.

Maria

18 November 1941

In Salvador and China, in Spain and Nicaragua
risings began.
                    Sandino said,
"When the people are satisfied with freedom,
let the ants bring me the news underground."
I could no longer use a camera—no one face,
no mass of sombreros was enough in number.
I was one of a mass whose horizon I couldn't see.
I focused on the daily task. I let love
set my limits, when I could. I let the body,
whose discipline is pain, choose a generous
death.
                    Now I was Maria,
Mexico's name for each of its alien poor.
I took the name, studied in Moscow, traveled
long roads in hunger. I said to the sun,
you lead me. Somehow a modest life grew.

We had a world, we said, to wash clean, minds
to renew. I was one of the many drops of rain
on the clear pane elegant tyrants erect as a shield
between themselves and the poor. This glass,
I felt, we will wash it clean, break through—
and if in the heat of love or hate
we dry on the glass—blood spatter, rain spatter,
wine—well, we do.
                    I was not afraid.

I lived level to the need to stop blood, carry water,
make soup. Before Spain, I loved best
the work away from desks, the wordless work
of fields and floors—digging or washing or gathering
wheat in. In Spain I lived with Carlos. I thought,
he has organized an army: his will. And I can still

see the 5th Regiment,

their caps thrown into the air, the last bars of
"La Internacional" lingering in the shouts to be on
with it, a massive surge of faces, blended and composed—
tidal music, centuries of repression breaking free
at last, we thought. It was a time that compares
to music, to a harmony of will and sacrifice so valid
it feels as if the world is spinning in your hand,
and in that rhythm we moved, firm in the principles
and demands of the time, inviting our ancestors, all
those who suffered, to be there in the impersonal
intensity of our blood. We had, for a time,
great power. And as always with great power,

we were tested.

Madrid

23 November 1941

In the first days of Madrid, when the city was the front,
Mamma was in my head—I couldn't get her out—
as if she'd given me her energy to use. I felt
protected. In a break in the bombing, so quiet
it seemed morning, I took keys to the supply room,
a pail and a mop, strangely happy—content
the way children are, not knowing why they're here
but sure of their right to be, not knowing how the world
unfolds but trusting the movement, the way I'd follow
close on Papa's whistle, not knowing the tune
but there with him note for note, as if I knew.
I splashed the stone floor with water, and they were
Udine's stones in the piazza when we cleaned
winter off and the barrels of last wine were rolled in.
The town was then one family. Today, Mamma teased,
everyone's papa is yours, everyone's husband is mine.
Work or no work, life was fine.

I flung the last of the water into a corner, between
cabinets, and then—I'd heard nothing, seen nothing—
I knew. I took the gun from my coat pocket,
demanding the shadow walk out of the shadow.
Three times, more. But he bolted, tumbled into me,
past me, stumbling at the door as I shot. He fell.
The blood welled, ran over his collar, filled
the cracks between stones, the crooked stones.
Stunned, I watched them fill, inch by inch—
the floor a map of Europe, this a school, these
the rivers down to the common sea.
                                        Who was he?
I searched him for papers. He was blank. Ours, theirs—
I never knew. Carlos said, "No matter.
Supplies are low. He was stealing food. You know
what the Party demands."
                                        I knew.

And this was the source of my calm thereafter:
I owed a death. My place would be filled.
I had reached the final edge of choice, and as
I stood there, ready in the larder that had been
Udine in spring and a sharing of wine, I willed
one thing only—purity intense as earth's,
a boundless cup into which all blood would sink,
valued equally, and by the compassionate chaos
of time lie hidden from view.
                              In me this was
sentiment. But in Badajoz, Seville, Granada—
fascists gave commands. *Limpieza*, purity so
impersonal, it was ironic, grand. "Give them coffee,
lots of coffee." Then a burst of shells, and cups,
coffee cups, thousands, shattered their brown blood
on the ground. On stones it drained, stained,
seeped from view. There was in the rhetoric
at dawn more blood. Loudspeakers spat it,
radios waved wet *banderas*, blood on the air,
and these rained down new rumor, blood in the streets.
Young men who rode trams to the front, women
in the factories heard of *limpieza*. Anarchist,
priest, communist—all of us knew this wish
for purity—that victims be invisible, be coffee
steamed into the ground.
                              Briefly I hated the dead.
Hated them, loved them, all in the dead man
at my feet. I held his blood in the lines of my hand,
watched it dry. Who was he? He was me. He was mine.
I needed the blood—here, in my hand. Stronger
than any caress, more mute, it said *yes*.
I was bound to claim him—
                              else be lost
in violence, too free, possessed.

The fascists stacked our dead,
El Mundo Obrero balled in their mouths,
the flesh of their most private moments cut off,
scattered. They were to be icons of our impotence,
syllables in a debate that daily grew unspeakable.

Carlos said—you are so silent.

I am, I said. Yes, I am.

From a Single Center . . .

21 December 1941

we tried to live. That's as it should be.
Now there's argument and doubt.
The center shifts, the line falls back, allies
unmask themselves, or mask. A few dry apologists
argue the war, they justify by numbers—how many
of ours were taken for *paseos*, how many of theirs;
how many cells were filled, emptied and filled,
by mistake how many; whether the ears
that hear confession now detect through their sleep,
faint and shrill, ululations the Africans made
when they fell on young women, how many at a time. . . .

What is counting but the wish for distance?
I counted, too—lentils, so scarce we doled them out
like pills; children who needed succor; Franco's
columns, four, and that mysterious fifth, the spies.
By Málaga I hoped never to see another war—
and then Guernica, Brunete, Teruel, Tarragona,
Barcelona yet to come. I could, in the last year,
no longer tell the color of an armband,
so many were blood, no longer measure loss
or honesty—they are not flour that sifts or bandages
that fold. They are open wounds down a corridor,
you want to close your eyes.
                              Lines that fled
the burning town I counted by cart and car and mile.
We had to be calm—was there time to feel?
My heart was sealed, a cask of wine let down a well
to keep from thieves, to age in the dark and cool.
Thirsty, or longing to be drunk, I'd send down
a grappling hook and hear the echo of a thump,
the scrape of stone and metal. Because I had learned
to hold a gun, to shoot, I saw in my hand,
as if in a smoking mirror or a lake burned off
by sun, the Aztec signature of war unfold,

the blossom at the tip of the detached god's bone.
You can't ask what is cruel or kind.

Was I blind?
          In the war I saw up close—so close
a mountainside of stark trees against snow could seem
an old man's face, unshaven. A rose was an urgent
smear, red down a wall. When we had time
for a personal love, Carlos and I,
we used our bodies like braille.

Events are our minds turned inside out.
In Madrid, in heroic November, the wounded
were loaded in on stretchers, in the trunks of cars,
or slung in carts like sheaves of torn hay.
In the kitchen a cauldron of thin garlic soup,
some beans. Bread came stale—in burlap sacks
long skinny loaves, floured "bones" without feet.
Their knobs blued with mold in the larder,
the leftovers stacked there, too tough for jaws
that stammered and mewed cold breath like gauze,
then locked in a final freeze of pain.
                              "Maria,"
they called—the urge for last words so strong
that almost, almost in the conscious ones I'd see
words gather speed, change, shake free
like sweat on muscle. Nearly impersonal,
finally beautiful, they told their last stories,
their lives, keeping alive in their whispers
what never can be lost. . . .

Sometimes there is no time—it cascades
and eddies, flows backwards, spews future, past,
and present in a mix. In San Martín, a jolt
of the ambulance over the ruts of the field sent me
a glimpse of a face—I saw a child, gentle and sad.

He belonged nowhere, and he stood exactly there,
in the red dirt, dried garlic looped in the window
behind him, the smoke on the white walls ashen.
He held a broken puppet by a string, something
human or animal carved from a gourd. I looked,
looked again, but had to go on—to Madrid,
to beds where young men left their words in blood,
where fever smudged the sheets with visions
of their children, born and unborn, orphaned
to the cradles of the mud.

If we could look into the future, would we go there?
In the spiral of hunger's discontent, would we go?

Somehow we go. New societies are born,
much wider than our minds. And if for a moment
we doubt, our bodies remember. They believe.
We make our bodies available to death,
and therefore live. It is the hero's way—

every woman knows it.

Retreat to the Future

1 January 1942

As the Republic's last Cortes disbanded,
and the stones of Figueras shook in the echo of bombs,
our people, frantic, were shoved from the winter roads
by our own troops, disregarded. They only watched
as national treasures, paintings huge in their gold
frames, took their places, cradled
in the last trucks going out. No one cried,

What have you done? What more can you give?

No theory marshaled the suffering of Spain
to right order. I felt its weight
as I watched in disgust. I felt love shudder
from power and change to an endless debt.
Offered a ride, I refused and walked the other way,
to the Plaza. There, I sat at a café table to wait—
for what?
        The town was empty. A bit of sun,
soured like the rind in the dirty glass on the dirty
table, was left. It hung limp on an ancient oak,
the city's center.

Through this Plaza men for the Brigades had passed.
Overhead a black bird screamed—the jolted
town an ambulance, stuck in a ditch.
I watched the shadows of the old oak lengthen.
My shadow stretched in the dust to sleep.
I closed my eyes and saw the after-lines of branches
turn blood in the cracks of crooked stones.
I wanted to float in these—I knew
where they went.
But I drifted down
to Udine, a day when Papa nailed wood at right angles.
He built a frame, stood it on end as if to ask
what next? what more? holding that window up to the sky,
squaring off part, the air lens enough,

the frame his telescope.
Then I drifted, years,
and in the darkroom this window of Papa's hovered,
parting known from unknown as a human face,
seen clear enough to honor, washed
mutely into view—
a beggar's gaunt face.
She didn't move her lips, but I heard her say,
"You will hang my sorrow on a wall?" She spat
and turned away. "Don't pray to it."

Startled, I shook
awake. I felt a sudden joy. I stood and felt
the muscles in my thighs—they were strong. I breathed
in, and in. I flung the dirty glass to the roots of the old
oak, watched it flash and shatter. And I followed
the people I loved across the border, a tatter of retreat,
refugees by the thousands crossing from Catalonia
to the French camps, to bitter charges,
countercharges—to the scourge of our better
natures, defeat.

When Carlos found me,
he had words from Machado ready on his lips—
Y cuando llegue el día del último viaje . . .
When the day of my last journey arrives,
and the ship, never to return, is set to leave,
you will find me on board with few supplies . . .
casi desnudo, almost naked, like the children
of the sea. He smiled, looked mostly ahead,
without reprisal, proud. "It is not our last
battle," he said.
                            Was he right?
Was there hope? I hoped. Arms limp at my sides
as he held me, too tired then to say or be anything
more than a bookmark closed in the book of his body,

the future unread. It was a relief
not to be dead—that strengthened me. Regret
is one blindness I've refused. Without that,
the least life is good.

I have seen light quicken
across silent faces, *de repente*, sudden as lightning
across a solid sea, then thunder stir deep passion,
and the dead—I mean
those who have lived without history, more silent
than fossils—awaken,
ready to live and die that their children might live
and die in dignity. They fix their eyes on that.

With such men and women I live.
And if it often seems we have the choice of fire
or fire, and the cities burn, the children scream,
and the war, a hired taxi with no driver, stalls
between burning walls and burning trees
in whose roots real serpents crawl—
I can grow still and wait
until Papa's frame floats up, a focus. Then I see
clear
              a simple human face.

I can follow that.

Home

4 January 1942

I have lived many lives since in Venice I saw
glassblowers shape to their fragile uses each angry breath.
Now the days come one by one—I predict neither
memory nor future.
                              Yet I have seen,
one twilight in Moscow, a piece of frozen river
ruffle up into the sky—ice as a pale blue rose
too distant for tether or root. I rubbed my eyes,
and the rose broke apart into whip-lines,
long arcs and V's—
                              and I knew they were swans,
perhaps wild geese, in their mass and sheer
movement amazing. Near the bridge where I stood
were skaters. They scored solid ice, their shadows
long behind them, moving into night. Above
and below, the world moved one way.
I have moved with it. That I know.

Where is my home?
My small life has touched lives in Italy, Los Angeles, Mexico,
Moscow, Spain. In them all I see the photograph
Edward took at Tacubaya—I'm sitting in a doorway
dressed in black, in our courtyard facing past a tree
and shadows on the wall. The wind that swept Mexico
is still, the dust is low.

Edward has set his tripod at a distance by the well
where he washes each morning. I dream
sun on the *azotea*, the dark room of a new life—
unaware of the pattern composed as he backs farther
away and stops down to so great a depth of field
that the door goes back into darkness forever.
That dark doorway I call home—

part of the dialectic we live.

Out on the street, lovers saunter, eating celery.
Azucenas spill from the windows. Churchbells, anvils,
roses ring in a single translation: *Vivid, la vida sigue.*
Live, for life goes on.
                    None of us has time for a single
life to stun the air as a flower can, fully realized.

Therefore we gather, en masse.

Notes to the Poems

Memories of the Future

In 1936, Spain was divided between those who opposed fascism, priests, landowners, the military, and the aristocracy and those who opposed Marxism, anarchism, labor unions, agrarian reform, and the untapped political power of the poor. When Franco and the Generals rose against the Second Republic, a civil war followed, and the forces in Spain that had been moving toward revolution were submerged in the struggle to defeat Franco and preserve the Republic. The triumph of a fascist dictatorship eventually resulted. Mussolini and Hitler aided the Generals; the Soviet Union aided the Republic. Although the United States, Britain, and to a lesser degree France remained neutral, fifty thousand volunteers from fifty-four countries formed International Brigades in defense of the Republic. Half of Spain's people died in the violence of this war—the first in which major population centers were ruthlessly bombed.

The idea that we choose our own deaths, and the quotation "Join love and power . . . ," both come from Friedrich Nietzsche, whose *Beyond Good and Evil* Modotti studied.

Doctrines of Glass and Wood

The uncle Benvenuto and the visit to the glass factories are not part of Modotti's life as documented in biographical sources.

The Kiss of Our Parents

The quasi-erotic nature of Modotti's relationship with her father is not documented in any biographical source.

Greed, a film directed by Erich von Stroheim.

Doors, Opening as They Do . . .

"I think I should begin to do some work . . ." and the remaining words quoted or paraphrased (ll. 11, 14–16, 18–19) are from Rainer Maria Rilke's *The Notebooks of Malte Laurids Brigge*.

For additional information on Edward Weston, see Ben Maddow, *Edward Weston: 50 Years*, and *The Daybooks of Edward Weston*, Volumes I and II, edited by Nancy Newhall.

Some of the descriptive phrases in lines 67–71 are influenced by passages from *Idols Behind Altars*, which Modotti knew well. The description of the serape echoes the words of the painter Jean Charlot, a friend of hers.

Fast Light

"Whose world is this . . ." is from Ezra Pound's Canto LXXXI, a poem Modotti referred to in a letter to Edward Weston.

In the Market

"Los muertos mueran . . ." is from Antonio Machado, the Spanish poet. See note to "Home" for the entire poem. Modotti knew Machado in Spain and cared for him as for a father. According to Vidali, Machado referred to Tina as "the angel of my house."

Still Lives

"Between living and dreaming . . ." is from "Proverbios y cantares," in *Campos de Castillo* by Antonio Machado:

Entre el vivir y el soñar
Hay una tercera cosa.
Andivínala.

The "invisible hand" is Adam Smith's way of describing metaphorically the concept that the marketplace is self-regulating under capitalism.

Franco brought the Moorish Regulares and the Spanish Foreign Legion (Tercios) from Africa to fight against the Republic. They were fierce and barbaric troops, given to mutilation and rape.

Vocation

"Me considero una fotógrafa . . ." is the opening sentence of a statement about photography that Modotti wrote to accompany an exhibition of her photographs. In the statement she speaks of her reluctance to use the term *artist* to describe her status.

Día de los Muertos

The Day of the Dead is the first two days in November when dead children and adults return to visit the living, a time of fiesta, with picnics on graves, and the stores and market stalls full of bread or candy skulls for sale.

For more information on Julio Antonio Mella, see Ernesto Dumpierre, *Mella*, and Raquel Tibol, *J. A. Mella in "El Machete."*

The "tyrant Machado" is Gerardo Machado y Morales, dictator of Cuba (1925–1933).

Maria

The risings, or the revolutionary attempts to gain political power, were the result of long histories of exploitation of the working classes and peasants. Some of the risings led eventually to political power for the oppressed; others did not. The revolution in El Salvador was crushed in the massacre of 1932. The struggle in China led eventually to Mao's victory and the formation of the Republic of Red China. In Spain, the revolt of the miners in Asturias in 1934 was put down by the Second Republic, itself headed toward civil war. In Nicaragua, Augusto César Sandino and his guerrillas resisted the presence of the U.S. Marines, laying down arms only when the Marines left the country. The Marine-trained National Guard and the Somoza family retained power in Nicaragua until the 1979 victory by the "Sandinistas" and others. Modotti had met Sandino in Mexico, volunteering to go to Nicaragua to help the guerrillas, an offer Sandino refused because of the harshness of guerrilla life.

Madrid

The scene in the supply room is not documented in any of the biographical sources.

El Mundo Obrero, the newspaper of the Communist party of Spain.

From a Single Center . . .

"Allies unmask themselves, or mask." Modotti spoke in private to Vidali of her opposition to the Non-Aggression Pact between Germany and the Soviet Union, signed August 23, 1939. Hitler's army invaded the Soviet Union on June 22, 1941, and was not defeated until after Modotti's death. She was aware that many Soviets who had worked in Spain during the Civil War were arrested or disappeared on their return to the Soviet Union, and she knew that the Soviet Union could not be a home for her or for Vidali. Like many Communists, she was unaware of the extent of Stalin's purges.

Retreat to the Future

The Cortes is the parliamentary body of the Republic of Spain.

These lines are the final stanza of "Retrato" ("Portrait"), in Antonio Machado's *Campos de Castillo* (my translation).

Y cuando llegue el día del último viaje,
y este al partir la nave que nunca ha de tornar,
me encontraréis a bordo, ligero de equipaje,
casi desnudo, como los hijos de la mar.

Home

Vivid, la vida sigue.
Los muertos mueran y las sombras pasan.
Lleva quien deja y vive el que ha vivido.
¡Yunques, sonad! ¡En medeced, campagnas!

Live, for life goes on.
The dead die, shadows pass.
He who leaves remains with us still; he who has lived, lives.
Anvils, ring! Be silent, steeple bells!

Antonio Machado

The verse is quoted in Hugh Thomas, *The Spanish Civil War* (Rev. ed.; New York, 1977), 196. Thomas cites Gerald Brenan as translator and alters that translation. I have offered a translation of my own.

Glossary

(Spanish to English unless otherwise noted)

aguacates—avocados

alameda—grove of poplars, park

avenida—avenue

azotea—flat roof

azucenas—lilies

banderas—flags

brasero—brasier, grate

campesino (-a)—peasant

comal—flat earthenware disk used for baking tortillas

compadre—godfather, a relationship of eternal friendship

cristallo (It.)—hard brittle glass

de repente—suddenly

Estoy un poco triste hoy—I'm a little sad today.

La Internacional—the "International," the anthem of the proletariat

limpieza—cleanliness, purity, honesty

madrugar—to dawn; (slang) to move fast, to take the enemy by surprise

maguey—cactus from which pulque, mescal, and tequila are made

maíz—corn

mescalito—mescal spirits, little god of the mescal

negrita—little dark one (a term of affection)

negrita cambuja—little dark half-breed (a term of denigration)

ollas—pots

panteón—cemetery

paseos—walks or rides. The kidnapped person taken for a *paseo* was usually killed.

petate—woven reed mat upon which humble Mexicans were born, ate, slept, died

presente—present, here

pulque—fermented juice from the maguey cactus

puta—whore

rebozo—a woman's shawl

rosetas—little roses; popcorn

51

Salud!—Greetings! Your health!

síntesis—synthesis

soledad—solitude

tiempo muerto—literally, dead time; the off-season in Cuba's sugarcane harvest, a time of unemployment and great hunger among the workers in an economy then controlled by foreign investments and foreign markets

títere—a puppet

vacilada—as described by Anita Brenner in *Idols Behind Altars*, a loud laugh combining faith and doubt, a sardonic cry in which all opposites are held

zafra—in Cuba, harvest